Zero Hour

"It's time, my children
When the waves rise high
When the waters run deep
When the clock strikes midnight
You'll feel the mark of Zero Hour
And you'll never be the same again"

~ Lisa Mangum
(The Hourglass Door)

Acknowledgments

The following poems have been previously published:

Grandmother Preserves, Sustenance anthology
(Anvil Press, 2017)

Color Wheel, Lemonspouting, 2021

Aeaea, Sunflowers,
The Lotus Tree Literary Review, Autumn, 2022

Visitations, B Movie Scenes,
Sea and Cedar Magazine, Winter, 2023

Chronology,
Quills Canadian Poetry Magazine, Vol. XII, 2023

Propagation,
Reedy Branch Review, Vol. 5, 2023

Zero Hour

Carla Stein

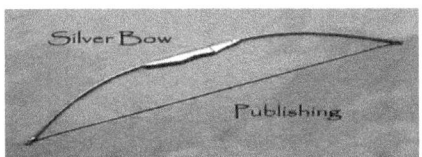

720 Sixth Street, Unit #5
New Westminster, BC
V3L 3C5
CANADA

Title: Zero Hour
Author: Carla Stein
Publisher: Silver Bow Publishing
Cover Art: "Relativity" by Carla Stein
Cover Layout and Design: Candice James

All rights reserved including the right to reproduce or translate this book or any portions thereof, in any form without the permission of the publisher. Except for the use of short passages for review purposes, no part of this book may be reproduced, in part or in whole, or transmitted in any form or by any means, either by means electronically or mechanically, including photocopying, recording, or any information or storage retrieval system without prior permission in writing from the publisher or a licence from the Canadian Copyright Collective Agency (Access Copyright).
© Silver Bow Publishing 2024

www.silverbowpublishing.com
info@silverbowpublishing.com
ISBN: 978-1-77403-305-0- paperback
ISBN: 978-1-77403-306-7 electronic book

Library and Archives Canada Cataloguing in Publication

Title: Zero hour / Carla Stein.
Other titles: Zero hour (Compilation)
Names: Stein, Carla, author.
Identifiers: Canadiana (print) 20240375726 | Canadiana (ebook) 20240375734 | ISBN 9781774033050
   (softcover) | ISBN 9781774033067 (Kindle)
Subjects: LCGFT: Poetry.
Classification: LCC PS8637.T436 Z18 2024 | DDC C811/.6—dc23

Zero Hour

For Ross and strawberry mysteries

Zero Hour

Contents

Mysteries / 9
Familiar and Strange / 10
my tongue speaks words i no longer hear / 11
To Lake Michigan / 12
Propagation / 13
Visitations / 14
Old Trunks / 15
Giraffe / 16
Pas de Deux / 17
Manoeuvres / 18
A Disposition / 19
Aeaea / 20
To Mama Doll / 21
Raw Milk / 22
Samson's Resort – an epilogue / 23
B Movie Scenes / 24
Perspective / 25
To a Silk Dress / 26
The Purpose of Perfume / 27
Traif Recollections / 28
Ripenings / 29
Genealogy / 30
Lenin Lives in La Grange / 31
A Poem for Frank / 32
Raisins / 33
Charlie / 34
Harvesting / 36
An Inquiry / 37
Grandmother Preserves / 38
Amends / 40
Haze / 41
Chronology / 42
Accretions / 44
You Escaped from Memory / 45
To an Aging Artist / 46
Sunflowers / 47
Berried Chimeras / 48
To Darva / 49
Rules of Engagement / 50
Convergence / 51

Sun Dogs and Open Toe Shoes / 52
Dawn / 53
We Picked Strawberries / 54
Leavings / 55
Happily Ever After / 56
Balloons / 57
Conversation with a Clothes Dryer / 58
Aix en Provence / 59
Neighbours / 60
An Errant Daffodil / 61
Sunday, Late February / 62
British Columbia Throat Songs / 63
Selfie / 65
fons et origo (source and origin) / 66
Fugue / 67
Colour Wheel / 68
Name Calling (for Sheri-D Wilson) / 69
Street Music / 70
Doggerel / 71
August / 72
To My Hands / 73
Recovery / 74
Zero Hour / 75

Mysteries

Paint me your negative spaces —

the liquid ones, less well-explored;
ignored for more solid avenues

Sing me the gaps —

between your words
the pauses between your sighs

Share your quiet corners —

where no time intrudes
on worlds far brighter
than these eyes foresee

Familiar and Strange

The maple tree stands steadfast. Sandy roads carve out property lines

we have come to claim the unwanted things

whose aches and needs took root?   e-e-e—motional
phantoms trail their sweet miasma / children,
fathers, mothers, assorted kith and kin

Daguerreotypes hidden in antique dresser drawers
sepia faces never encountered in life, their names —
guessing games >

childhood curiosity crowded out /
                transparent borders frame
figurines of flat-faced dogs /
                witness disrupted descendants

      What If —
muddy stems / linger?

We must decide the fate of fancy dishes,
scalloped edges, dancing women
in porcelain gowns — cracked and sorrowful
under layered dust

resolve
b-b-b—looms beneath
my reddened bandage

in giant seashells
held to ears
the ocean roars

my tongue speaks words i no longer hear

my grandmother does not visit my sleep
I never knew boundaries of the woman
I knew masked before I was who we knew
each together for a time not the whole of her time
       in the times we knitted comfort
         shaped as socks, sweaters,
an intricate crochet of hours amidst flapping laundry
brining pickles kneading challah ironed bed sheets
       potatoes dressed in sour cream
       chicken plucked, roasted anatomy —
learned recipe by recipe that lives in my bones
lives in my daughter's glasses balanced on her nose

To Lake Michigan

Your winter white caps etch my dreams.
I am in love with your hieroglyphs. intaglio
inscribed on frozen sand. effaced again at waking.
your January pebbles forge cement.
salt-free hands paint your frigid watercolor surface.
ten thousand sunken freighters,
bowriders netted by swift currents,
fish boats tossed in your chop.
fear rides your shifting bottom.
summer mornings reflect across your face.
midday magentas dye your rip tides,
fade into ochre nights while cricket serenades
swaddle sand-crusted alewive skins.
you rippled secrets to my childhood ankles.
welcomed my sun-warmed body into liquid mirrors,
        glistened, teased.

    I squander a sleeping breath.
    recall wisps of floating weed.
    you are not known for kindness

Propagation

squares of deer fence sag on their rebar posts.
the weight of hedgerows
pushing, pulling them askew.
her face mask slipping off nose and lips
still smiling though hips are pulled askew;
her weight supported
on a steel cane and motorized cart;
the season behind what warmth it should bring.
the ponds unaffected by sun bear no algae.
the parrot's feather, water hyacinth struggle.
elodea canadensis stifled;
unlike the rushes and papyrus she has potted
waiting on a small table to hitchhike to new homes
in the midst of concrete angels, bowls,
pagodas pock-marked with acid rain –
a testamentary to years she farmed these alien ponds
on land that never spoke her tongue.
she's sure anything can be invasive
if you feed it enough snacks

Alberni Highway barn —
funky steel frog gulps mildew

Visitations

You can still find the place
where the cottage lived. You can still close
tired eyes and transport into dry summer grass,
humid sun, mosquito-filled nights,
still feel scraped knees burning with iodine,
hear admonishments to stay off cottage roofs,
stare back at faces long gone.

You can still observe a frog
picture the one you kept in a jar, how you
fed it captive flies, sent it back to the trees
when you thought it looked sad.

You can still smell crisp cucumbers, garlic,
dill weed bathing in salt brine,
impatient fingers dipping in
to snatch a taste of pickles in the making.

You can still draw your name
with pointed toes
in sea-shelled sand
you pretend surrounds
a much-loved lake
where the cottage lived.

Old Trunks

A need for tidiness compels storage.

Organizing previous chaos — an illusive goal at best —
leads to rectangular containers
stuffed with non-necessities:

Monopoly games that lack pieces, not memories

*Crocheted throws that offer threads
from grandmothers' lives*

*A canvas backpack
boasting unadorned collegiate odors*

*A ski cap and mittens,
longing for head and hands to warm*

Brochures mapping roads long since diverted

*Faded album covers
pounding out melodies too scratched to play*

Barely ordered worlds,
existing in heartbeat and synapse,
safely, mutely concealed,
between four walls and a lid.

Giraffe

Though her fingers have
never winnowed African soil
her hand strides the Serengeti
with a long-necked puppet —
stitched legs stretched
across continental rifts

aware of lion jaws, yet unafraid
its spotted head prunes leaves
entwined in periwinkle skies —

the hope of childhood dreams
reflected in a glued-on eye

Pas-de-Deux

a delicate configuration
intro'd the dinner dance
potatoes peeled and cut
with a diva's finesse as

her understudy flic flac-d
the diva's flowered skirt
above wrinkled knees
in counterpoint to the waltz
between sink and stove

a gas burner boiled water
choreographed bubbles
the pot lid percolated
tympanic rhythms

the danseuse voiced
staccato warnings
scalded nightshades drained
steaming liquid kissed porcelain

penché-d off a cherished spoon
melted butter and milk
fouetté-d with tubers
into perfect starchy peaks

the coda opened
to little feet in pas de chat
around the kitchen table

understudy's hands in demi-bras
fingers en face to forks and knives
supper places set

Manoeuvres

sweet peas taunt a private rave in pinks and mauves.
across a sand crusted road the green stems dance,
purpled scents dare trespass.

sun tanned mothers, aunts recline
at grandmother's cottage.
don't notice an eight-year-old practice espionage
before a petal-trampling invasion.

feet wade into trailing shoots.
hands pick one stem, another.
fingers palm a polychrome bouquet.
the wasp lands.
my arm swells.

tall grass waves
branches dip
peaches fall

A Disposition

my grandfather and Mr. Wilson
exchanged handshakes
pulled chairs up — side by side
leaned on the long sunroom table
        allowed to stay, wordlessly I watched

catalpa leaves sway
three p.m. light glints off tea-filled glasses
served Russian-fashion, hot and strong
jam-dipped spoons stir, sweeten the brew
        familiarity reclaimed formality

"Will, how's business?"
"Good, Abe."
then banter — weather, politics
swatted mosquitoes
catch-ups on children, contracts renewed
another season settled
        child eyes Kodachrome'd

each parched face
each worried life framed
in heavy-lidded stares
gray-flecked heads held firm
shoulders stiff with pride
        on a single thick plate

brittle cookies beckon both men
my grandfather's hand,
carameled by a Michigan summer,
Mr. Wilson's ebony palm
        a parallel reach shared

sugared circles dipped in tea,
shared jokes about
the challenges of dentures,
the pulling of teeth
in Black and Jewish mouths

Aeaea

Beauty acknowledged you
made immortal promises
love sustained, sheltered, only by *Beauty* —
her solitary alabaster arms wrapped
you in honey-ed air
unbound a sexless silken veil
as you fed on her island illusions

Beauty's warmth and *Beauty's* smile —
her fruits ripening forever
the table piled with pledges while
Beauty spoke her truth
made you a lie
gave you a world and
took your freedom

To Mama Doll

your voicebox nestles
in your cotton-stuffed belly

you never compare my almost black hair
my midnight irises to your blonde curls
your blue-glazed eyes

you repeat your faith in me again and again
as my fingers press your core

Raw Milk

Smuggled memories of the old country
in a mason jar —

a gnarled finger hushing lips:

"This for your grandmother. Our secret."

his farm boots brushing
sun-dried grass, striding
toward the cottage door:

"Fresh from my cows. Don't tell."

butterfat-laden fluid sloshed
beneath a thick cream cap —

when I asked to taste some / she answered:

"Not for you. It's not safe."

Samson's Resort – an epilogue

eight sneakered feet
kick dust on roadside
sweet peas
        wasps hide in perfume

we swear secrecy
purloin piggy bank coins
plot a concession store invasion

small hands stifle giggles
tongues imagine
orange crush bubbles
        nickel miracles wilt in sunbeams

ice cream sandwiches
fudgesicles, peanut-crusted
coronets drip as

eight sneakered feet
skid into knee high grass
revive a rusty playground
        swing sets sway

a merry-go-round creaks
beckons legs to leap
hands to push

see-saws bounce
childhood cheers
balance on blistered paint
        shuttered buildings hover

windows vacant
rogue cousins twist
weathered doorknobs

eight sets of fingers
seek signs of children
long grown and gone

B Movie Scenes

beach days spark violet illusions —
a heat-born mirage with Elizabeth Taylor eyes
        joins the squish
         of wet sand
         through toes
that stampede on National Velvet hooves,
              pausing
where water nuzzles land to hurl
a sunbaked child, arms soaring, face splashed,
a rider of little belly waves,
who barely hears shore-bound voices
appeal for eight-year-old caution,
repeat a *don't go in too far* litany,
bellow *you don't know how to swim* heresies

before beach shoes hammer across hot sand
while you and Elizabeth gaze
on lake bottom stones and sunlight shards,
urge bursting lungs forward,
and stand in a violet winner's circle.

Perspective

in fear's shiny glare,
summer raindrops
mimic a deluge

To a Silk Dress

Unlike the midnight of my mother's hair
where reddish highlights flashed,
your dark-spun larval strands
drank daylight, consumed
her hands' gentle caresses

You absorbed the sweep
of six-year-old eyes, tolerated
my borrowed dress-up dramas

She called you 'shirt-waist',
twirled your ebony sleeves,
your subtle folds, thin
as the bones of her palms
thin as her olive-skinned arms

Your moonless skirts
circle my dreamscapes, the way
your loosened buttons revealed
her fairy-wisp clavicles,
her subtle sorrows,
blacker than your threads

The Purpose of Perfume

I never saw the rose —
only its essence distilled
carefully captured in clear glass
capped tightly and kept as
memento of his eyes
pouring through pages
at a reference library table
his hands fixed on frantic scribbling,
cramped from stubby pencils

the yellow brown elixir
nested among transparent flasks,
tubes, bottles of unknown content
a chemist's menagerie trapped
in a locked enamel cabinet
the rose waiting for grandfather
hands to unscrew the lid —
waft its telltale fragrance
toward my curious nose

Traif Recollections

before she got religion
or religion got her —
there was Dairy Queen

before slick seats
or blizzard confections
there were hot-footed toes
on a baked sidewalk

behind glass
a hot dog-studded carousel
offered blistered foot-longs
dripping grease over an electric bonfire
and our small mouths mostly ordered
frozen custard cones that sweated
a challenge to keep
chocolate or butterscotch shells from
a slide toward unforgiving pavement

before parents' dictates chose for her
my eight-year-old cousin demanded,

"Mustard – only mustard."

watched the sausage drop into a
pool of yellow spice, reached
up to pull a napkin-wrapped bun
through the pass-through window

while a smiling teen leaned down,
joked the sandwich
was bigger than the kid —

and we took bets
that she wouldn't eat it all

Ripenings

that summer, the cottage pear tree
proffered shrunken limbs
held out a promise of fruit
that never appeared

aunts and uncles disdained
the trunk's tattered look
bark harshed gray with
too much sun, too little rain

that summer, his memory almost as barren,
my gray-harshed grandfather
defended twisted, knobby branches

heedless of uncles
worried over roots in septic pipes
aunts' distaste for yellowed leaves

his grizzled hands hauled
discards from the refuse bin
dug peach peels, cantaloupe, corn husks,
the fruit of unremembered meals,
into sandy earth near tree roots,
blessed the work with pails of water

his distant heat-filled recollections
like random cream on milk gone sour
poured silence on voices who muttered
about more sleep, more medication,
whispered he was as ruined as the tree

that winter, watermelon rinds,
onion skins, apple cores rotted while
my grandfather forgot fruit trees
forgot cottages and corn husks
became a memory we tasted
in next summer's ripened pears
picked from shrunken limbs

Genealogy

These mothers, draped in peonies and promise
unfurl oxygen-painted skirts
rabbits on their laps nestle in chlorophyll patterns
They croon, *"Come, be close."* —

wrap children in quilts of lacewings and clover
conduct bee concertos among
columbines and wild carrot
brush milkweed floss against infant cheeks.

These fathers, dressed in mold and mushrooms,
spit geysers, juggle meteors, maggots
lean rock-slide limbs on wildfire canes
dare, *"Come, dine with me."* —

offer hydrogen-heaped plates
garnished with galactic gyrations
suffering and starlight; swipe
moonbeams across young eyes

These uncles carry seaweed-speckled capes
joust with sharks, swordfish, squid
tumble toward water-logged canyons
spray salted breath upon scions' hair

These cousins preen airy vests
flounce indigo, vermillion wings
glide ultramarine updrafts
crow confetti choruses

These grandmothers, aunts
glaze despair onto my lips
wear habits of sorrow
pad along concrete pathways
feet tangled in dollar-store discards

Lenin Lives in La Grange

Lurking among the tree-lined streets
Lenin spits as Ford Falcons overflow with kids
driven to school, piano lessons, sleepovers,
clenches his fist
at this instant mashed potato bourgeois comfort ...

He paces the commuter station
watchful between trains for thin ties,
beige trench coats – the latest FBI disguise
hard to spot agents concealed amidst all
the other thin ties and trench coats.

"You need to live the capitalist experience
firsthand, to defeat it.", Aunt E. insists
Lenin striding by her side, quietly nods
as she deftly dodges the latest Bureau tail.

Aunt E. knows the enemy, keeps books for the man,
reads the Daily Worker, disapproves of Trotsky,
venerates Paul Robeson,
has joined the N double-A-CP
supports the League of Women Voters
parlays about oppression to immigrant laborers.

Cuts her hair in a fashionable bob,
shops for skirts at Evan Picone,
frequents the floors at Marshall Field's,
purchases a camel-colored cashmere overcoat,
buys designer shoes to march on May Day
for the imminent revolution.

Lenin, skeptical, but trusting her dedication,
invests in khakis, loafers, golf clubs,
argyle socks, pullover sweaters.
He shaves the beard. Stops shouting at crowds.
Comes to love Baskin-Robbins.
Thinks seriously about owning a thin tie.

A Poem for Frank

"I will write you a poem," she said.
And to his blank stare added,
"Because I don't have patience for a novel."

And so she wrote his future twenty years ahead.

Wrote how they would barely remember this night
standing at the festival doors
exchanging anecdotes of past performances
and former professors.
Each story grander than the first.

Wrote how three kids in the back of a hybrid SUV
and three more years left on the mortgage
would leave him blankly staring at a notebook
she left behind, when there was
no more patience for poems.

Raisins

little balls of dried life
warm in my hand
nourish my presence
in wrinkled folds.

Charlie

I.

Charlie was an ageless fable
older than we could say
in summers when we were small
his suspenders yanked gaunt shoulders,
a gray beard brushed his shirt collar,
stained pants hung above mud-caked shoes
his yellow teeth peeked
from a tobacco-cured smile.

> *The septic tank is leaking.*
> *The pump is broken.*
> *Go get Charlie!*

We welcomed any excuse
to spy inside his crumbling cabin
plank shelves stacked with canned goods
his quilt-strewn metal bed wedged
between wall and woodstove

We pretended to ride his twin-cylinder
Indian propped against his paint-chipped door ...
Charlie shoo-ed us off; flaunted his
I mean business face — we giggled.

Thick glasses over misty blue eyes,
cap crowning unruly hair, toolbox gripped tight,
his skilled motions convinced the pump to sputter,
the water tank to fill.

Grandfathers and uncles
offered handshakes,
poured lemonade
into sun-warmed glasses

II.

Charlie wavered
with the lake-born breeze
in summers when we had grown
we carried leftovers
to his home, watched
him roll cigarettes,

listened to his motorcycle memories;
counted tumbled machine parts
among the weeds in his yard.

We asked parents
if he would be alright in winter
when we were city-bound.

We wondered about the sadness
grown-up faces tried to mask,
wondered why Charlie
ate his dinners alone

Harvesting

Cigar-like pods dangle. Each one
Announces summer turning her page
Tantalizes ten-year-olds with smoking aspirations
Alters laundry poles into gathering tools wielded by
Lithe bodies who leap toward
Pliant leaves, knock branches, bruise limbs,
Achieve the ability to wound a tree.

An Inquiry

I can't see the finish line
along this unmarked route

the present elides a shrouded path
peopled by fallen comrades, lovers,
old friends with forgotten names

their faces float in dreams,
point the way back like fabled crumbs,

dissolve into laugh-filled memories
stowed away on waking

I pack bags lighter though they grow heavier
photos, greeting cards, printed notes,
scrawled letters addressed to ghosts,
find me at this twist, this living litany, chanting

"Repeat the route 'til you know it by heart."
my pulse sings the rhythm while muscles riff along:

Did I get the words right?

Zero Hour

Grandmother Preserves

I told myself I'd write it down —
would keep a record of
the way she decided
blackberries balanced sugar

whether crabapples, raspberries
or pears would be a good addition
how long to boil them together,
the trick to knowing jars were sealed

methods crafted by mother,
aunts, etched in her visual guide.
        no wordy details.
intoned instructions: *Just watch*

Did her mother whisper: *Watch*
as fathers, uncles, chose shovels,
picks, and rakes to counter hard-eyed hatred

Did her aunt admonish: *Watch*
whether jars of jam, bushels of wheat,
sacks of flour would trick
or seal a Cossack's bloodlust

Who did she watch sailing toward
streets paved with gold; city districts
located by whether gooseberries
or green grapes graced a peddler's cart

Who looked on as she calibrated
English consonants to Yiddish vowels,
marched with unionists, dodged nightsticks,
sold peppermints, fed depression-hungry
sons and daughters; lost everyone
who had not sailed.

Blue and black berries slowly simmer
in my kitchen, sugar added —
just enough to set the fruit. Jars clean,
ready to fill, soft cloth handy to wipe lids.

Zero Hour

between stirs I observe roil
and thickening, notice dark syrup,
skim lighter foam;
monitor temperature.

notebook and pen at hand
I begin writing it all down,
    imagine she is...
             watching.

Amends

The house sits unreadable
no expression from doors, windows
plush rugs, brass handles

we enter through new locks
her accusatory walls wrap without warmth
there's no welcome in her vestibule

she's the mother whose empty womb
won't take us back
won't sooth our errors
erase our missteps

we circle her with fawn lilies, gum weed
plant blue iris grass, scouler's willow;
bald hip roses watch a blank sky
reflect in her dust-caked panes;

we pray for rain
cry no tears
the water is too precious

Haze

      rain
on January mountains

    fog hides snow
memories blur your face

Chronology

lips move phrases within
a lacuna of days,
a concise vocabulary notes
sparrows at the feeder
chides a dog, a cat —
intervals dissolve

bruises transit inward, fade to yellow

week-long downpours cohere
a wheelbarrow rain gauge
drizzles constellations
spilled, poked
a wane sun enters

spider webs know home and comfort

machine motions redeem contamination
pump hot water, soap minutes
clothes fold into dog walks
scrubbed pans bake dinners
brownie-buttered fingers
grease a shopping list

raisin-dry life warms my palm

window ledges announce dust
the vacuum sucks in shortbread crumbs,
a carrot slice the dog didn't want
cat hair frosts the Bauhaus chair
chartreuse curtains flutter
the cat jumps in the clothes hamper
considers a nap, jumps out

well-stitched seams contain joy

streetlights glow too soon
I contemplate condensation
could thicker windows shield damp?
I design interior space additions —

Zero Hour

who would live there?

no crannys for random thoughts

linens freshen, pillows fluff
curtains pull against chill
book opens, pages turn
the cat cuddles
I wrap in tight blankets,
sweeten with night sweats

foggy mornings resurrect frosted nights

muffins will be baked
with September cranberries, orange peels

forgetting it's December
snapdragons, dianthus bloom

worms, woodbugs
will chew plum leaves, twigs
into next spring's compost

a concise vocabulary will assure, assure

a concise vocabulary assures

all flowers may be everlastings

Accretions

Lux et misericordia
light and compassion drips.

Drips the candle wax stalagmite on the table,
trickles hosts of silent dusk into dark.

Fingers filter tears as mouths weep
breath-filled fog onto chilled glass.

There is softness in shared pain —
and sometimes, peace.

You Escaped from Memory

I wonder about you. Wonder at the years
since we shared a Dodge van
cramped with six explorers of inner space,
vapors of mystical incense passed from hands,
to lips, to lungs, then passed again.

Hitch hiking on the road to yourself,
you'd entered that rust-battered door;
we sat thighs pressed to elbows while tires rolled,
shoveled words, uncovered contrivances,
mined the stuff of years in 24 hours.

When Wyoming painted a red rock horizon
with sunrise, you whispered
you might find yourself in her hills.
Our driver stopped — the brown door slid open.

We stood together
on roadside shingle.

You said come with me.

I needed to find an ocean.

Now your name
has vanished in her waves.

To an Aging Artist

obsidian eyes
round black baby eyes
fringed in wrinkles
when you smile and

when you smile
a toddler's too full cheeks
stretch across a grown man's jaw

stretch cinnamon skin
soft little boy's skin pitted
with stubble, hard, black

your moonstone teeth
milk white children's teeth
bite dark into eroded lips

as you hide your years
long wine-spice years
beneath a costume-cowboy's hat

Sunflowers

all winter
I watched them wither
heads bowing deeper
with each snowfall

they grew more quickly
than the corn we planted —
lacked proportion,
a parody of our emotions

today their frost-burned tops
rattle in a spring-scented wind

in my hand, fresh seed packets
foretell a crop of daydreams
in a summer cornfield

Berried Chimeras

grandmother knits
blueberries, cherries, grapevines
an elixir for what ails...

she dips her needles
into indigo juice ...
hands skitter in a forget-me-not haze,
mix with strawberry-pinks,
watercolor stains float

landscapes of wool
clicked and clacked
into stocking-stitch garments

her berry-flavored yarns
warm me 'til morning

To Darva

rapt in your waiting
he will enter blue rooms
hold you rose-perfect
between searing hands

lost in his loving
you will whither sun-dry
float like parched grass
before blown kisses

adrift in this ending
you will paint walls red
he will search for rain

Rules of Engagement

in this bedded moment,
so unlike a marriage bed

we inhale broken vows —
so like marriage beds

that mash long nights,
hard days beneath the bedded
residues we bring to those beds
that wrap our skins — so like marriage beds

with their wine-fueled stares afloat on beds
of fearless-feather words, virgin covenants,
the bedded moments we exhale –
not unlike a marriage bed

Convergence

where lines converge
there is a place
you have not named

mapping the boundaries of
our bodies by
perimeters of affection

we become voyageurs on
rivers of silence,
dig channels for sweat
through fenced-off flesh
privatized by promises
navigated by remorse

rivers rise with snow melt
etch their own
history on parched land
dictate a route you have yet to learn

shout lines to dam their flow
rivers will not hear you
will not heed you,
will spill into a place
you'll label *Change*

Sun Dogs and Open Toe Shoes

Minus thirteen Celsius
and this morning's Island forecast
brings back thoughts of you, Saskatchewan —
of a me naïve to block heaters and remote starters
wind chill factors that count down
seconds to freeze bare skin
whiteout warnings ignored
that end in frozen bodies
only ten feet from a truck and

me, only a few months arrived from the Coast,
on a long past February morning
a day the sun dogs growled in a too blue sky —
the parking lot swept clean
by the constant wind
I stepped into the office
sporting my kick-heeled sandals
my almost-spring Island thoughts
drowned by a chorus of co-worker gasps and

you, my parka clad knight, you
asking if I was crazy, running out
to plug in the block heater
lecturing on frostbite, sun dogs, ice crystals
as you squeezed my fingers
took care that I stayed warm

Dawn

crouched on new mown grass
two rabbits lick dew
my pursed lips dust your cheek

We Picked Strawberries

in a nearby field —

sticky rivulets bright red as blood
stained little mouths

four pairs of hands — filled buckets
*laughter and sweat
overflowed*

one more fruit
found lips instead of pail

sun-baked white blossoms
stuck to our fingers

the farmer cautioned
step between the rows

we sat cross-legged in the dirt
ate most of the harvest

small hands — now big
*filled with newly picked
delights*

your hands — remembered
in this jam-jar poem

Leavings

You are still here
while I sit in summer-less sun
wearing your black T-shirt —
      too big and
full of tiny holes from
too many washings

the fat November starlings
clamber on the brown bark feeder
you left here last July —

I see you twist your green silk scarf
wrap it round
your sweat-damp brow —

now I only wrap it
'round the wind.

Happily Ever After

I dreamed you over and over
not believing the story

my dream said you were there
a traveler looking for me

I searched for the story's ghost
re-wrote the ending in my dream

found you a hundred times —

never saw your face

Balloons

cups
filled to tears
float sorrow

helium dreams
slip from
children's wrists

Conversation with a Clothes Dryer

light streams through fabric
once resplendent with rainbows,
unicorns, promises of magical dreams

its threadbare lens frames
your cartwheels across our front lawn
your mischievous toddler smile,
your age-six tongue licking
sugar from an ice cream-less cone

I catch my breath. Replay you
perched on a branch too frail
to hold your chimera motion,
as you instruct crows
to eat fallen cherries

I feel your warm pillowcase
flitter through my fingers
washed so many times
it's gossamer now,
thin and threatening to tear

Aix-en-Provence

The streets here are like
The shoreline at home –
Rocky, uneven, but without the ocean.
Here a sea of tobacco-tinged people
Rush over the stones,
Their tides dictated only by
The heat of day and the cool of night.

J'ai peur de tomber en amour
With this place where *je suis*
Étranger mais pas estranged.
Where Cézanne saw and was not seen.
Where the walls are thick
And people dance in the streets.
Where the barred windows stripe your view
And the sun lulls you to sleep.

J'ai peur de partir d'ici et
J'ai peur de rester.

There are fountains here,
But no place to swim,
Leaving tired men to soak their
Feet in man-made waterfalls
While the coffee flows
In the street corner cafes
And the dog urine flows
Along the street corners.

J'ai peur de tomber en amour
With the grey green olive leaves
And the orange ochre buildings,
Avec le marché, des fleurs, des aubergines,
The cheeses, *des tomates, la crème glacée,*
And the smoke-filled men.

J'ai peur de tomber en amour and
I fear I have forgotten how.

Neighbours

Nose to grass and mud
or held high into the wind,
my dog reads sticky notes, text messages
written in urine and pheromones.

Passing other pets and their tethered people,
he pauses to comment
on today's tree bark embedded blog post.

Recognition developed
through respective furred companions,
I nod to my fellow two-legged residents;
my canine escort multi-tasks
between signs of squirrel and deer.

An older gentleman waves
while puffing cigarette smoke.
A matron yells un-motherly sounds
stills her small pups that bark hello.
The cul-de-sac gardener urges my hound
to chase rabbits out of his azaleas.

Transiting neighbourhood cyberspace,
we ask the names of our dogs,
seldom volunteer our own,
type out tentative code with
four paws and a wagging tail.

An Errant Daffodil

pushing thin green arms toward
a drained December sky
she defies fog, freezing rain;
shouts a promise in citrine petals,
mirrors a hidden sun.

Sunday, Late February

The eagles have returned.
I awake groggy, hear their
trademark morning trilling

from the high wind-battered fir.
Mated for each other's lifetime,
this pair has raised a decade

of offspring. A few have stayed
in the neighborhood, added their
young majesty to the aerial ballets.

Through spring, summer, fall
my garden becomes a flyover;
new babes recognized by

still brown heads — snowy feathers
appearing only with maturity.
I glance away

from washing at the bathroom sink,
take note of milky silver tresses
now occupying half my head.

Someday, I'll untie pure ivory strands,
they'll float on thermal breezes —
marry white feathers.

British Columbia Throat Songs
(A Super Natural Weekend Adventure)

First set: the gig

We walk down Commercial Street, my daughter and I.
Look for a place to dine. My suitcase
rolls behind like a recalcitrant puppy.

The Drive is full of flashy signs, flashy storefronts,
flashier people, flailing arms and words,
figuring out how to spend Friday night.

We dodge dogs leashed, waiting.
Tied to bike racks and parking meters,
they keep solitary vigil over squares of pavement.
Their owners indulge the evening's itinerary.

One amalgam of terrier and Chihuahua,
whose mother may have been consort
to a French bulldog, stands by the curb.
Unremarkable, except for the capped
and bearded man crouched by the pug-ish head,
whispering thrumming noises
at transfixed fido eyes.

We smile, walk on — dinner awaits.
The suitcase catches on sidewalk cracks.

Second set: encore

Early spring light fades. Coffee shops close.
Patrons trade caffeine for beer and weed.
We re-trace our cement trail.
My suitcase obediently follows.

Skateboarders fly past.
Couples jam restaurant doorways.
Late night markets spill orchards of offerings
into boxed rows.
Mondrians of apples, bananas, broccoli
entice last minute shoppers.

Zero Hour

The crouched singer now stands mid-sidewalk,
fruited squares a backdrop to
the canine-focused concert.
Rounded lips shape his cavern-mouth.
The leash hangs loosely.
Rumbling decibels flood fur-tufted ears.

Tones move up and down a scale lost to logic,
emanate from feet, from belly,
climb through concrete,
plummet like Icarus' wings,
rise again as waterspouts.
Dance like angels on a follicle of dog hair.

        Coaxed to stillness
      by this crooning spectacle,
          we examine mangoes

Selfie

your face
in a cell phone's pixilated kingdom
a universal epiphany
that embodies digital sainthood
complete with thumbs up
and red hearts
that worship

your tongue feasting on chocolate gelato
your feet propped on a '57 Chevy
breakfastin' at a Florida beach
laughin' in a mid-downhill pose
stylin' a Yankees' ball cap
chillin' with tequila shots

software smoothes harsh edges
brightens eyes, releases backgrounds
from messy details

the worry lines
and curbside litter
the residue of sleepless nights

the tears running down your cheek

fons et origo (source and origin)

A poet, not quite boy, not yet man,
shares in the writing circle.
Poems of cattails, cypress, season's change.
Love of antelopes and avocets.
The wonder of lenticular clouds.

His work read, he holds ready
an antiquated fountain pen.
Listens to gray-haired verses,
presses his silver-tipped nib to paper.
      Ink flows.

words from old lips
hover in brightening mist
rain falls on young trees

Fugue

The old wooden ladder stands,
like Dave, before the laurel hedge.
Holding his hand saw, he climbs its steps
on legs that seem as frail as the wood,
yet hold him steady.

Foliage and branches hit the ground in near silence.
Dave, examining his work, shouts across to me,
"What's your dog's name?"

For the third time in as many days,
I say the name. And Dave, again mutters,
"I only have your dog to talk to."

> *dew drops dance*
> *refract sun's rays*
>   *air ripples*

Colour Wheel

The fence is the color of white noise
there to dampen the whine of a
neighbor's saws,
the clang of hammers, to hide
brown dirt-caked stumps of cedars
shredded in a paean
to suburban curb appeal

Daylilies spill like orange earplugs
gladiolas lift their salmon fish-lip petals
drink in crystal droplets sprayed
from a metal-gray hose

As my eyes watch liquid surcease
blacken garden dust
I say kaddish for the cedars

Name Calling
(for Sheri-D Wilson)

My name is an un-singable decibel
my other names are witch, mother,
siren, slut, sandstorm, sea foam,
serpent, silence

My sorrow is life
the third rail leap
the lightening sundered branch
the child grown-up too soon

She said come more often
I stabbed my shoeless toes
on my shredded poems
along her pathway

Until she came with her witch's broom
whisked the shards away
so I could *spell* words
dispel my fear
love the page

Could rip the sounds from my dreams
crush the name of my jazz-mother
charleston my hips into the mouth of a wolf

Roll on her tongue
sleep in moss-covered corners
drool over territories
of dead reindeer and cosmic sheep

drip dewdrops
from my wolf teeth marrow
tell her, I will always hear you
even if I never come.

Street Music

Mick Jagger is busy producing TV
about Mick Jagger
with Martin Scorsese

meanwhile, in Vancouver,
Rock and Roll is
Howling down the street
shaking up the passers-by
telling everyone,
listening, or not —
how much he hates Mick Jagger

'cuz Rock and Roll
is not invited to the party
with Mick and Martin

he's on the sidewalk
in front of Nordstorm's
bashing out
his love and hate
on his real-deal six string

he knows betrayal
like a rolling stone
knows that music's
in the concrete
as much as in the Vinyl

Doggerel

he points his eyes
to the shelf above,
ears raised to
pyramidal peaks

we know he covets the red ball

still, we joke –
If only he could talk ...

while all along he has been fluent
in the language of each muscle, hair, and bone

his integrated speech,
unencumbered by the
discords our words inflict

perhaps, he thinks,
If only they were silent.

August

John McCain lies in state
his star-spangled casket damp with tears
    while elsewhere
an erstwhile groupie, named Bill Clinton,
opines his memorial to Aretha Franklin

And I?
I am here to watch two young ravens
    chase the sky
glimpse an acrobat red squirrel
snatch acorns from a Garry oak;
marvel as Magritte clouds fold the sun

To My Hands

you are
my soul's touch
you commune with the world —

grasping, tapping, holding
stroking a babe's cheek
caressing a lover's open lips
wiping startled tears from
a child's eyes,
ladling festive soup
to a waiting family —

you carry time
grip smooth black pens
write words of gratitude

Recovery

Rabbits, raccoons, mice welcome
    carved-out spaces.
    Conduct a life there.

Buttercup and daphne creep
in barren gardens, crowd out
What If and *Why Not* seeds.

I imagined the possible.
You constructed details.

Beside a hollowed apple tree,
wants and needs have taken root.

Blackberry thorns
tear fingers
hungry for forgotten fruit.

I bite an apple's tardy sweetness,
    wonder if the cuts will scar.

Zero Hour

in a parallel universe
time may run backward
conjure a summer breath

a scientific tabloid decrees

I might bake again
in Michigan sunbeams
toss powdered sand
twitch dune grass
as bobwhite mutterings reanimate
on swelling crab tree branches

a scientific tabloid decrees

I might bend a heat-dazed book —
hawk-eye ants
who crawl over
humid letters, notice
letters mimic ants

pussy willow humming
might melt caution
so I refuse belief
in rattlesnakes —
until one holds sentry
on a neighbor's doorstep

a scientific tabloid decrees

time may roll backward
back to blackberries buzzing
whippoorwills and milkweed silks
canary light poured
through shuttered eyes

in a parallel universe
I might hear you call

whose words would answer?

Zero Hour

www.ingramcontent.com/pod-product-compliance
Lightning Source LLC
Chambersburg PA
CBHW052205070526
44585CB00017B/2076